— THE UNTOLD STORY OF —

MICHAEL COLLINS

APOLLO 11 PILOT

BY MARCIA AMIDON LUSTED

CAPSTONE PRESS
a capstone imprint

Published by Capstone Press, an imprint of Capstone
1710 Roe Crest Drive, North Mankato, Minnesota 56003
capstonepub.com

Library of Congress Cataloging-in-Publication Data
Names: Lüsted, Marcia Amidon, author.
Title: The untold story of Michael Collins : Apollo 11 Pilot / by Marcia Amidon
Lusted.
Description: North Mankato, Minnesota : Capstone Press, an imprint of
Capstone, [2024] | Includes bibliographical references. | Audience: Ages 8 to 11
| Audience: Grades 4-6 | Summary: "People don't usually remember Collins.
He's been called the "loneliest man in humanity" and the "forgotten astronaut."
But Collins was an important part of the Apollo 11 mission. If something had
happened to Armstrong or Aldrin, he would have had to rescue them. And he
was the only one who could bring them all home"-- Provided by publisher.
Identifiers: LCCN 2022047894 (print) | LCCN 2022047895 (ebook) |
  ISBN 9781669015949 (hardcover) | ISBN 9781669015895 (paperback) |
  ISBN 9781669015901 (pdf) | ISBN 9781669015925 (kindle edition) |
  ISBN 9781669015932 (epub)
Subjects: LCSH: Collins, Michael, 1930-2021--Juvenile literature. | Space flight
to the moon--Juvenile literature. | Project Apollo (U.S.)--Juvenile literature. |
Astronauts--United States--Biography--Juvenile literature.
Classification: LCC TL789.85.C65 L87 2024 (print) | LCC TL789.85.C65 (ebook)
| DDC 629.450092 [B]--dc23/eng/20221206
LC record available at https://lccn.loc.gov/2022047894
LC ebook record available at https://lccn.loc.gov/2022047895

Editorial Credits
Editor: Ericka Smith; Designer: Kayla Rossow; Media Researcher: Svetlana
Zhurkin; Production Specialist: Katy LaVigne

Image Credits
Alamy: imageBROKER, 6; Dreamstime: Mmphotos2017, 23; Getty Images:
Camerique, 11, sierrarat, 7; NASA: cover, 5, 12, 13, 15, 17, 19, 20, 21, 22, 24, 25,
26, 27; Shutterstock: Al Teich, 29, Julia Khimich (background), cover (right) and
throughout, Nadegda Rozova (background), cover (left) and throughout, Vadim
Sadovski, 9

All internet sites appearing in back matter were available and accurate when
this book was sent to press.

TABLE OF CONTENTS

Words in **bold** are in the glossary.

THE LONELIEST MAN IN HUMANITY

It was July 20, 1969. The Apollo 11 astronauts had reached the moon. Edwin "Buzz" Aldrin and Neil Armstrong landed on its dusty surface. Soon, they would take their first steps there. It would be the very first time humans walked on the moon.

Michael Collins stayed in the **command module**. It was called *Columbia*. In it, he **orbited** the moon while Aldrin and Armstrong explored its surface.

People don't usually remember Collins. He's been called the "loneliest man in humanity" and the "forgotten astronaut." But Collins was an important part of the Apollo 11 mission. If something had happened to Armstrong or Aldrin, he would have had to rescue them. And he was the only one who could bring them all home.

You've probably read about Armstrong's first steps on the moon. Here's the story of one of the astronauts who helped make that possible—Michael Collins.

Collins in a model of the command module before the Apollo 11 mission

FOLLOWING IN HIS FAMILY'S FOOTSTEPS

Collins was born in Rome, Italy, on October 31, 1930. His father was a United States Army general who had been **stationed** there. When World War II began, the family moved to Washington, DC. Living in Italy was no longer safe.

Rome, Italy, around 1930

Collins tried to fly this type of airplane while in Puerto Rico.

Later, Collins's father was sent to Puerto Rico. There, Collins took his first ride in an army plane. The pilot even let him fly the plane for part of the trip. After that, Collins decided he wanted to be a pilot.

Collins also dreamed about going into space. Mars was his favorite planet. He had read a lot about Mars and wanted to go there. After his trip to the moon, he joked that the National Aeronautics and Space Administration (NASA) had sent him to the wrong place.

Collins wanted to be in the military too. His father, uncles, brother, and cousin had all served. After high school, Collins went to West Point Military Academy. He graduated in 1952. Then he joined the U.S. Air Force.

FACT West Point Military Academy is a college for training U.S. Army officers. It was founded in 1802. It is located on the Hudson River north of New York City.

Mars and its two moons

LEARNING TO FLY

After joining the Air Force, Collins began training as a fighter pilot. He was so good that he began to fly jet fighters. Jet fighters can fly up to 1,550 miles (2,494 kilometers) per hour, so fighter pilots have to be able to think and act quickly to fly them.

Collins was also part of a bomber team. He learned how to deliver **nuclear** weapons. And he later became a test pilot. His job was to test new jet fighters and suggest improvements.

In the Air Force, Collins spent more than 4,200 hours flying. This experience helped him become an astronaut.

Air Force jets flying in formation in the mid-1950s

Collins thought he would keep flying jets until he saw the Mercury-Atlas 6 mission on February 20, 1962. That's when he decided he wanted to be an astronaut. He wanted to go into space like John Glenn Jr. During that mission, Glenn had orbited Earth three times in 4 hours and 55 minutes.

That same year, NASA was looking for more astronauts. Collins applied. He took physical and mental tests, but he was rejected. NASA said that he did not yet have the special skills to be an astronaut.

The launch for the Mercury-Atlas 6 mission

John Glenn Jr. next to the Mercury-Atlas 6 mission spacecraft *Friendship 7*

But Collins decided to keep trying. The Air Force was beginning to study space. They had created the Air Force Aerospace Research Pilot School. Collins joined the school to learn more about space. The school had a space flight simulator. In it, pilots could experience the sights, sounds, and feel of flying in space.

In 1963, Collins applied to NASA again. This time, they accepted him for astronaut training. As a part of his training, he had to learn survival skills. He also learned more science, including geology. And he had to learn how to move in **zero gravity**.

Astronaut Survival Training

Astronauts have to learn how to survive in case their space capsule crashes somewhere. When Collins trained as an astronaut, they were taken to deserts, to jungles, out into the ocean and left there. They learned how to find food and shelter. And they learned how to use the things that would be in the space capsule to help them survive.

Astronauts during a survival training in 1963

HIS FIRST MISSION

After Collins completed his astronaut training, he was ready for his first mission! In 1966, NASA chose him to be the pilot for the Gemini 10 mission. The mission's purpose was to show that a spacecraft could **dock** with another one while in orbit.

During the mission, the astronauts would also attempt a spacewalk—go outside of their spacecraft. The astronauts on the previous mission had trouble spacewalking. Collins would have to prove that he could do a better job.

John W. Young (left) and Collins of the Gemini 10 mission

Gemini 10 went into space on July 18, 1966. It docked with a spacecraft named *Agena*. It had been launched right before *Gemini 10*.

Collins's first spacewalk was just standing up so that part of his body was outside of the spacecraft. Then, he took pictures of space. Later, Collins went on a spacewalk to the *Agena*. He became the first person to visit another spacecraft in orbit. He was also the first person to spacewalk twice.

Three days after its launch, *Gemini 10* safely splashed down in the Pacific Ocean.

The mission also set a record. It was the highest **altitude** ever reached during a space flight—476 miles (766 km).

Young (left) and Collins aboard a U.S. Navy ship after their landing

TO THE MOON

In 1961, President John F. Kennedy had set a goal for the United States. He wanted to send a man to the moon and bring him safely back to Earth. To achieve that goal, between 1961 and 1969, NASA had more than a dozen manned missions to space. Through these missions, NASA learned how to build better spacecraft. And astronauts learned how to do more and more in space.

Armstrong (left), Collins (center), and Aldrin of the Apollo 11 mission

The Apollo 11 mission would achieve President Kennedy's goal. On July 16, 1969, Aldrin, Armstrong, and Collins were launched into space. Just a few days later, they would make history when Armstrong and Aldin would become the first astronauts to walk on the moon.

The Apollo 11 astronauts reached the moon on July 20, 1969. Armstrong and Aldrin flew to the surface of the moon in the **lunar module**. It was called the *Eagle*. It landed on the moon, and the two astronauts walked on the moon's surface. They collected rock samples and took photographs.

Collins stayed in the *Columbia* and orbited the moon for more than 21 hours. Collins could talk to Aldrin and Armstrong down on the surface of the moon through his radio. But for about 48 minutes during each orbit, while on the dark side of the moon, he was all alone with no radio contact.

Aldrin working next to the lunar module

Neil Armstrong and Buzz Aldrin Walk on the Moon

People often remember only Armstrong and Aldrin when they think about Apollo 11 because they walked on the moon. Armstrong was also the first one to step foot on the moon, and he spoke the most famous words from the mission: "That's one small step for man, one giant leap for mankind." Hundreds of millions of people around the world watched this moment on their televisions.

Collins stayed in orbit about 60 miles (97 km) above Aldrin and Armstrong on the moon's surface. His role was just as important. He was the only one who could fly the command module by himself. He would also have to rescue the other two if something went wrong with the lunar module.

Collins practices for the Apollo 11 mission in a command module simulator.

When the lunar module lifted off from the moon's surface, it met Collins in the *Columbia* while it was in orbit. Collins docked with the lunar module. Then, they went home.

The lunar module moves toward the *Columbia* to dock with it.

FACT Aldrin and Armstrong left behind an American flag, a patch in honor of the Apollo 1 crew, and a plaque on the moon. The plaque reads, "Here men from planet Earth first set foot upon the moon, July 1969 A.D. We came in peace for all mankind."

Getting back to Earth was not easy. The *Columbia* was traveling at 36,194 feet (11,032 meters) per second when it reached Earth's atmosphere. No one knew if they would survive.

Everyone had to wait a long nine minutes with no radio contact before the module came into sight. Its three parachutes landed it gently in the Pacific Ocean, southwest of Hawaii, and a ship picked up Aldrin, Armstrong, and Collins. They had made it home safely.

In recognition of their accomplishment, Aldrin, Armstrong, and Collins received the Presidential Medal of Freedom from President Richard Nixon in August 1969. They also received the Congressional Gold Medal in 2011.

The Apollo 11 crew waiting to be picked up after landing in the Pacific Ocean

Apollo 11 Wins the Hubbard Medal

The Apollo 11 astronauts received the National Geographic Society Hubbard Medal in 1970. It is awarded for research, discovery, and exploration. Fifty years later in 2020, Katherine Johnson received the award for her work on the mission. She calculated the flight paths for the Apollo 11 mission. It was her work that made it possible for the astronauts to make it safely to space and back.

Katherine Johnson

CHAPTER FIVE

A TRUE PIONEER

Collins never went into space again. In 1971, he became the first director of the Smithsonian's National Air and Space Museum in Washington, DC. He later worked for an aerospace company. And he wrote books about space—one was about the Apollo 11 mission.

Collins died on April 28, 2021, but he left quite the legacy. He was always willing to help push space exploration a bit further, whether it was walking in space or piloting the first trip to the moon. He played a key role in our journey to better understand a world that not long before had been beyond our reach. NASA called Collins "a true pioneer."

FACT Collins always believed that people should keep exploring space and other planets. He said, "It's human nature to stretch, to go, to see, to understand. Exploration is not a choice, really."

Michael Collins, 2019

GLOSSARY

altitude (AL-ti-tood)—how high something is above the Earth's surface

command module (kuh-MAND MOJ-ool)—the crew's quarters and flight-control section of an Apollo spacecraft

dock (DAHK)—to join two spacecraft together in space

lunar module (LOO-nuhr MOJ-ool)—the self-contained part of the larger spacecraft that landed on the moon

nuclear (NOO-klee-ur)—having to do with the energy created by splitting atoms; nuclear bombs use this energy to cause an explosion

orbit (OR-bit)—to travel around an object in space; an orbit is also the path an object follows while circling an object in space

station (STAY-shuhn)—to assign to work in a certain place

zero gravity (ZEER-oh GRAV-uh-tee)—the feeling of weightlessness that astronauts experience in space

READ MORE

Buckley, James, Jr. *Michael Collins: Forgotten Astronaut.* New York: Aladdin, 2019.

Halls, Kelly Milner. *Apollo 11 Q&A.* Emeryville, CA: Rockridge Press, 2021.

Schyffert, Bea Uusma. *The Man Who Went to the Far Side of the Moon: The Story of Apollo 11 Astronaut Michael Collins.* San Francisco: Chronicle Books, 2019.

INTERNET SITES

Kiddle: Michael Collins (Astronaut) Facts for Kids
kids.kiddle.co/Michael_Collins_(astronaut)

National Geographic Kids: The Moon Landing
kids.nationalgeographic.com/history/article/moon-landing

PlanBee: Moon Landing Facts for Kids
planbee.com/blogs/news/moon-landing-facts-for-kids

INDEX

ABOUT THE AUTHOR

Marcia Amidon Lusted has written 200 books and over 600 magazine articles for young readers of all ages. She also writes and edits for adults and works in sustainable development. Visit www.adventuresinnonfiction.com for more about her books.